CLASSIC ROCK
SHEET MUSIC

PlayList

SONGS THAT ROCKED THE WORLD!

Alfred Music Publishing Co., Inc.
16320 Roscoe Blvd., Suite 100
P.O. Box 10003
Van Nuys, CA 91410-0003
alfred.com

Copyright © MMIX by Alfred Music Publishing Co., Inc.
All rights reserved. Printed in USA.

ISBN-10: 0-7390-6201-8
ISBN-13: 978-0-7390-6201-2

CONTENTS

TITLE	ARTIST	PAGE
All Along the Watchtower	Jimi Hendrix	4
Black Water	The Doobie Brothers	10
Born to Run	Bruce Springsteen	16
Both Sides Now	Joni Mitchell	26
Can't Find My Way Home	Blind Faith	30
Comfortably Numb	Pink Floyd	63
Crazy Love	Van Morrison	38
Dear Mr. Fantasy	Traffic	42
Don't Stop Believin'	Journey	48
Good Times, Bad Times	Led Zeppelin	52
Great Balls of Fire	Jerry Lee Lewis	58
Hotel California	Eagles	68
I Can See Clearly Now	Johnny Nash	76
Just What I Needed	Cars	80
Layla	Derek and the Dominos	83
Like a Rolling Stone	Bob Dylan	170
Lola	The Kinks	90
Margaritaville	Jimmy Buffett	96
Na Na Hey Hey (Kiss Him Goodbye)	Steam	100

CONTENTS

TITLE	ARTIST	PAGE
Right Now	Van Halen	102
Roundabout	Yes	110
Running on Empty	Jackson Browne	126
Shower the People	James Taylor	134
Stairway to Heaven	Led Zeppelin	138
Sunshine of Your Love	Cream	150
Taxi	Harry Chapin	154
Time of the Season	The Zombies	166
Tom Sawyer	Rush	175
The Trees	Rush	182
Uncle John's Band	Grateful Dead	192
The Weight	The Band	199
Werewolves of London	Warren Zevon	208
Whipping Post	The Allman Brothers Band	202
A Whiter Shade of Pale	Procol Harum	215
Wish You Were Here	Pink Floyd	236
You Can Leave Your Hat On	Randy Newman	220
You Can't Always Get What You Want	The Rolling Stones	226

ALL ALONG THE WATCHTOWER

Words and Music by
BOB DYLAN

Moderate rock ♩ = 112

1. "There must be some kind of way

out - ta here,"___ said the jok - er to the thief.___

* Original recording: all guitars tuned down a 1/2 step in Cm.

© 1968 (Renewed) DWARF MUSIC
Used by Permission of MUSIC SALES CORPORATION (ASCAP)
All Rights Reserved

6

Verse 2:

BLACK WATER

Words and Music by
PATRICK SIMMONS

Lyrics: Well, I built me a raft ___ and she's read - y for float - in'; ol' Mis - sis - sip pi, ___ she's call - in' my name. ___

© 1974 (Renewed) WB MUSIC CORP. and LANDSDOWNE MUSIC PUBLISHERS
All Rights Administered by WB MUSIC CORP.
All Rights Reserved

12

dif - fer - ence— to me; just take that street - car that's go -

in' up - town. ___ Yeah, I'd like to hear some fun - ky

Dix - ie - land— and dance — a hon - ky - tonk, — and I'll be

buy - in' ev-'ry-bod-y drinks— all 'roun'. ____

D. S. 𝄋 al Coda ⟐

BORN TO RUN

Words and Music by
BRUCE SPRINGSTEEN

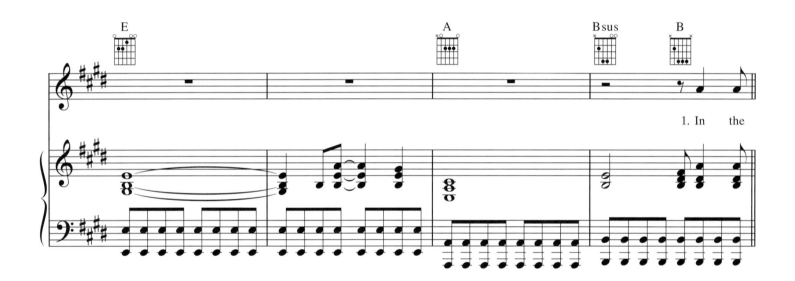

Born to Run - 10 - 1

© 1975 (Renewed) BRUCE SPRINGSTEEN (ASCAP)
All Rights Reserved

2. Wen - dy,

Sax. solo:

Be -

Bridge:

yond the Pal - ace, hem - i - pow-ered drones_ scream_ down the bou - le - vard._

_ Girls comb their hair_ in rear - view mir-rors and the

boys try to look so hard. The a - muse-ment park_ ris - es

bold and stark_ as kids are hud-dled on the beach in the mist._____ I wan - na

die with you, Wen-dy, on the streets to-night__ in an ev-er-last-ing kiss.___ *Huh!*

One, two three, four! 3. The

Verse 3:

high-way's jammed_ with bro - ken he - ros on a last - chance pow - er drive.

Ev - 'ry - bod - y's out on the run_____ to-night, but there's

no place left to hide.____ To - geth - er, Wen - dy, we can

BOTH SIDES NOW

Gtr. tuned to "Open E":
E-7-5-4-3-5

⑥ = E ③ = G#
⑤ = B ② = B
④ = E ① = E

Words and Music by
JOBI MITCHELL

Both Sides Now - 4 - 1

© 1967 (Renewed) CRAZY CROW MUSIC
All Rights Administered by Sony/ATV Music Publishing, 8 Music Square West, Nashville, TN 37203
All Rights Reserved

Verse 3:
Tears and fears and feeling proud,
To say "I Love You," right out loud
Dreams and schemes and circus crowds
I've looked at life that way
But now old friends are acting strange
They shake their heads, they say I've changed
Well, something's lost, but something's gained
In living every day.

Chorus 3:
I've looked at life from both sides now
From win and lose, and still somehow
It's life's illusions I recall
I really don't know life at all.

Chorus 4:
I've looked at life from both sides now
From up and down, and still somehow
It's life's illusions I recall
I really don't know life at all.

CAN'T FIND MY WAY HOME

All gtrs. in Drop D tuning:
⑥ = D ③ = G
⑤ = A ② = B
④ = D ① = E

Words and Music by
STEVE WINWOOD

Moderately slow ♩ = 88

Verse 1:

down off__ your throne_____ and leave your bod-y a-lone._____

© 1970 (Renewed) F.S. MUSIC LIMITED (PRS)
All Rights Administered by WARNER-TAMERLANE PUBLISHING CORP.
All Rights Reserved

and I'm___ wast - ed___ and I can't___ find my way___ home.___

Ooh.___

Chorus 2:

CRAZY LOVE

Words and Music by
VAN MORRISON

Slowly ♩ = 72

Verses 1 & 2:

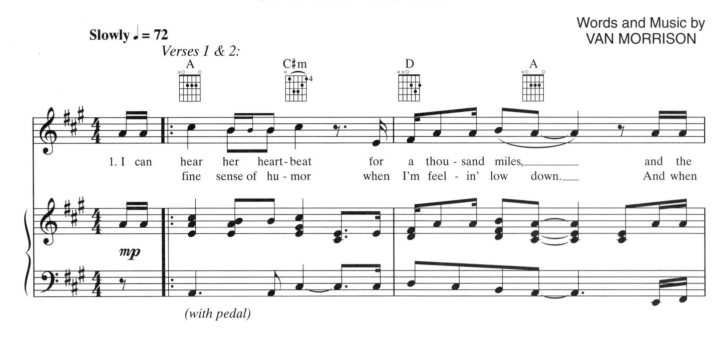

1. I can hear her heart-beat for a thou-sand miles,_____ and the
   fine sense of hu-mor when I'm feel-in' low down.___ And when

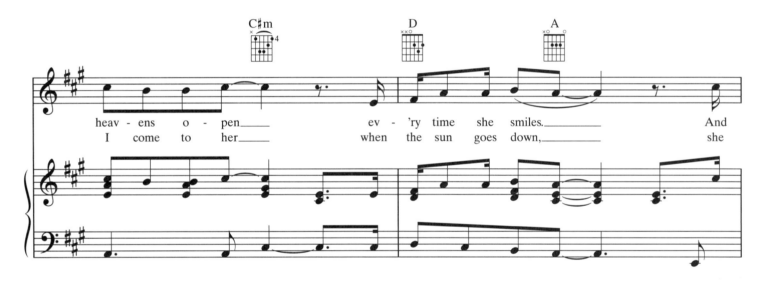

heav - ens o - pen_____ ev - 'ry time she smiles._____ And
I come to her_____ when the sun goes down,_____ she

when I come to her, that's where I be-long._____ Yes, I'm
takes a - way my trou - ble, takes a-way my___ grief.___ Takes a -

Crazy Love - 4 - 1

© 1971 (Renewed) WB MUSIC CORP. and CALEDONIA SOUL MUSIC
All Rights Administered by WB MUSIC CORP.
All Rights Reserved

41

Chorus:

Crazy Love - 4 - 4

DEAR MR. FANTASY

Words and Music by
STEVE WINWOOD,
CHRIS WOOD and JIM CAPALDI

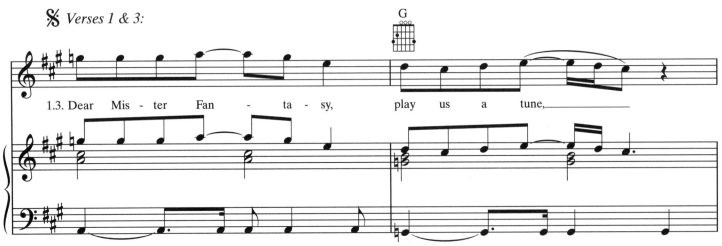

1.3. Dear Mis- ter Fan- ta- sy, play us a tune,_____

© 1968 (Renewed) F.S. MUSIC LTD. and ISLAND MUSIC LTD.
All Rights For F.S.MUSIC LTD. Administered by WARNER-TAMERLANE PUBLISHING CORP.
All Rights Reserved

Coda

Instrumental solo ad lib.:

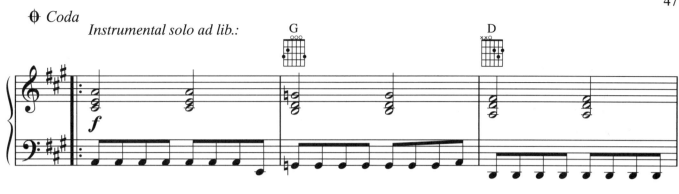

Play 5 times

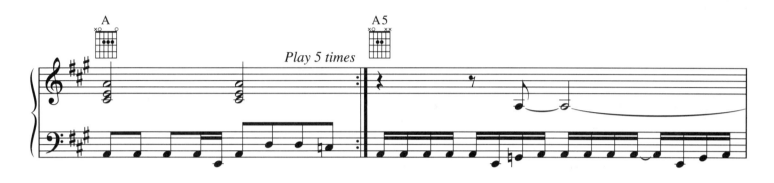

Repeat and fade

DON'T STOP BELIEVIN'

Words and Music by
JONATHAN CAIN, NEAL SCHON
and STEVE PERRY

© 1981 WEEDHIGH-NIGHTMARE MUSIC and LACEY BOULEVARD MUSIC
All Rights for WEEDHIGH-NIGHTMARE MUSIC Administered by WIXEN MUSIC PUBLISHING INC.
All Rights Reserved

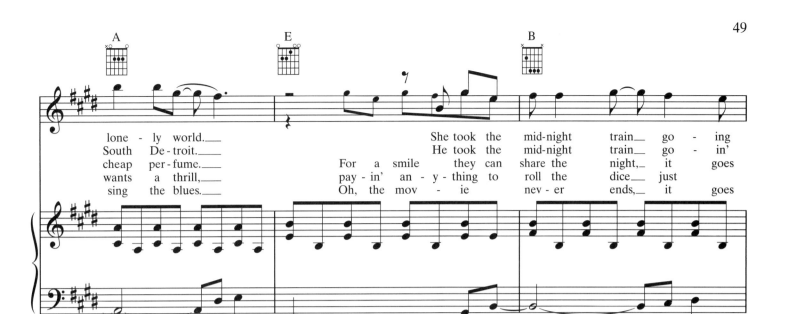

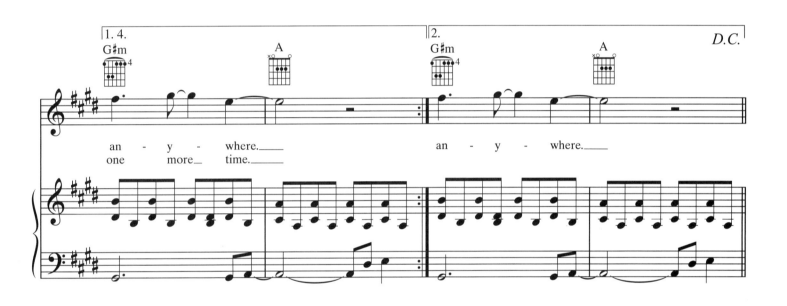

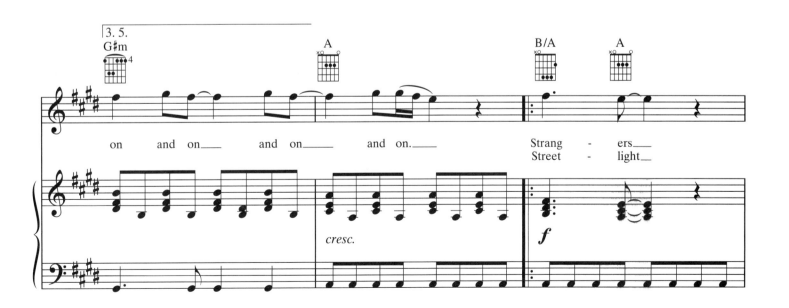

GOOD TIMES, BAD TIMES

Words and Music by
JIMMY PAGE, JOHN PAUL JONES
and JOHN BONHAM

Moderate rock ♩ = 96

Verse:

In the days of my youth, I was

told   what it   means___   to   be   a   man.___

Good Times, Bad Times - 6 - 1

© 1969 (Renewed) FLAMES OF ALBION MUSIC, INC.
All Rights Administered by WB MUSIC CORP.
Exclusive Print Rights for the World Excluding Europe Administered by ALFRED PUBLISHING CO., INC.
All Rights Reserved

Chorus:

Guitar solo:

Guitar solo ad lib.

Chorus:

Good   times,   bad___ times,___   you know I've   had   my   share.___   Well, my

Ad lib. vocal:
I know what it means to be alone,
I sure do wish I was at home.
I don't care what the neighbors say,
I'm gonna love you each and every day.
You can feel the beat within my heart.
Realize, sweet babe, we ain't never gonna part.

GREAT BALLS OF FIRE

Words and Music by
OTIS BLACKWELL and JACK HAMMER

Rock and roll ♩ = 152

Great Balls of Fire - 5 - 1

© 1957 (Renewed) UNICHAPPELL MUSIC INC., MIJAC MUSIC, CHAPPELL & CO., INC. and MYSTICAL LIGHT MUSIC
All Rights on behalf of itself and MIJAC MUSIC Administered by UNICHAPPELL MUSIC INC.
All Rights on behalf of itself and MYSTICAL LIGHT MUSIC Administered by CHAPPELL & CO., INC.
All Rights Reserved

To Coda

sure is fun.___ C - 'mon, ba - by, you're driv - ing me cra - zy.

Piano solo:

Good - ness gra - cious, great___ *balls of fire!*

COMFORTABLY NUMB

Words and Music by
ROGER WATERS and DAVID GILMOUR

Slowly ♩ = 66

Verse:

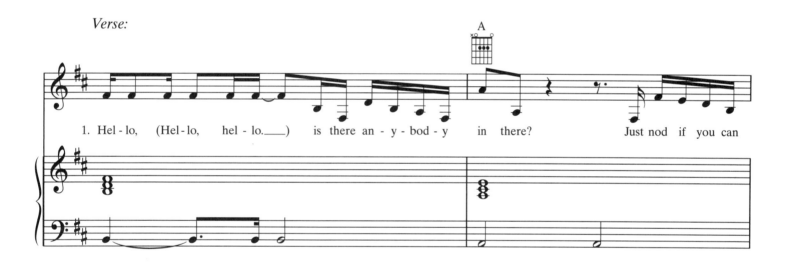

1. Hel - lo, (Hel - lo, hel - lo.___) is there an - y - bod - y in there? Just nod if you can

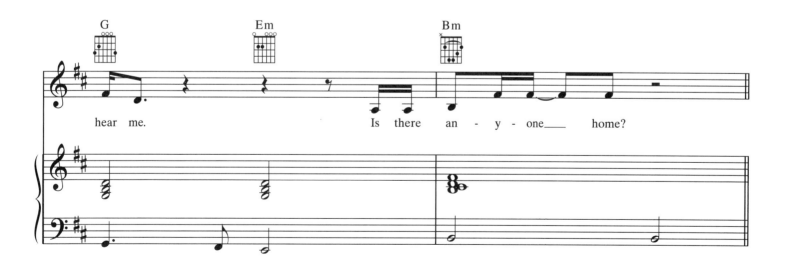

hear me. Is there an - y - one___ home?

Comfortably Numb - 5 - 1

© 1979 ROGER WATERS OVERSEAS LTD.
All Rights for the U.S. and Canada Administered by WARNER-TAMERLANE PUBLISHING CORP.
All Rights Reserved

Come on, now,_____ I hear you're feel - ing_____ down.___ Well,
(Come on, come on.___)
2. O - kay, (O - kay, o - kay.___) just a lit - tle pin - prick. There'll be no more...

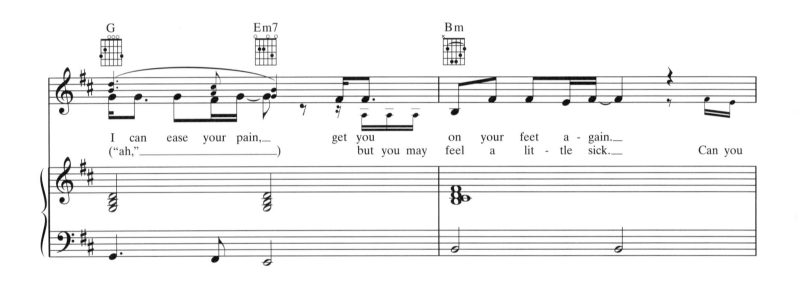

I can ease your pain,___ get you on your feet a - gain.___ Can you
("ah,"_____) but you may feel a lit - tle sick.___

Re - lax, (Re - lax, re - lax.___) I need some in - for - ma - tion first.___
stand up? (Stand up, stand up.___) I do be - lieve it's work - ing. Good.___ That - 'll keep you

HOTEL CALIFORNIA

Words and Music by
DON HENLEY, GLENN FREY
and DON FELDER

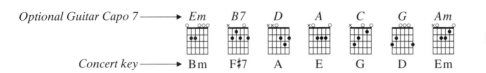

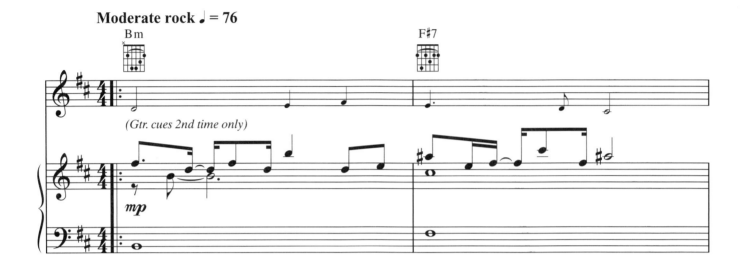

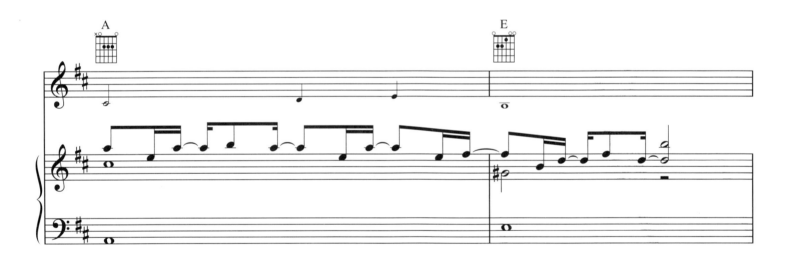

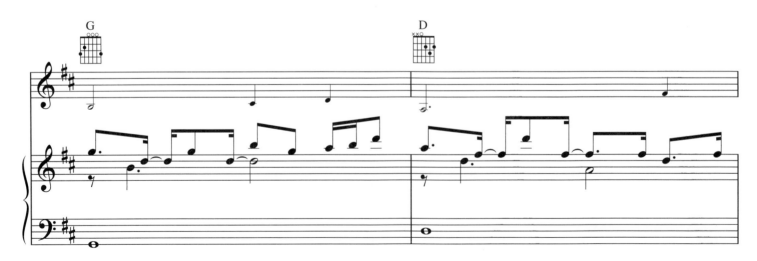

Hotel California - 8 - 1

© 1976 (Renewed) CASS COUNTY MUSIC, RED CLOUD MUSIC and FINGERS MUSIC
All Print Rights for CASS COUNTY MUSIC and RED CLOUD MUSIC Administered by WARNER-TAMERLANE PUBLISHING CORP.
All Rights for FINGERS MUSIC Administered by WB MUSIC CORP.
All Rights Reserved

Verses 1 & 2:

1. On a dark des-ert high-way, cool wind in my hair,
2. Her mind is Tif-fa-ny twist-ed, she got the Mer-ce-des bends.

warm smell of co-li-tas rising up through the air.
She got a lot of pret-ty, pret-ty boys that she calls friends.

Up a-head in the dis-tance, I saw a shim-mer-ing light.
How they dance in the court-yard, sweet sum-mer sweat.

they gath-ered for the feast. They stab it_____ with their steel - y knives,_ but they

just can't___ kill the beast. Last thing_ I re - mem - ber, I was

run - ning_ for the door. I had to find the pas-sage back_ to the

place I was_ be - fore._____ "Re-lax," said the night - man. "We are_

I CAN SEE CLEARLY NOW

Words and Music by
JOHNNY NASH

Reggae ♩ = 120

% *Verse:*

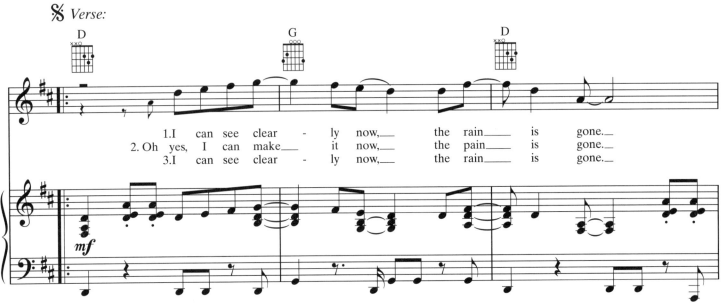

1.I can see clear - ly now,___ the rain___ is gone.___
2.Oh yes, I can make___ it now,___ the pain___ is gone.___
3.I can see clear - ly now,___ the rain___ is gone.___

I can see all___ ob - sta - cles___
All of the bad___ feel - ings have___
I can see all___ ob - sta - cles___

© 1972 (Renewed) NASHCO MUSIC
All Rights for the World Outside of North America Administered by WARNER/CHAPPELL MUSIC, INC.
All Rights Reserved

Bridge:

Look all a - round,_____ there's noth - ing but blue skies._____

Look straight a - head, there's noth - ing but

blue skies._____

JUST WHAT I NEEDED

Words and Music by
RIC OCASEK

Medium Rock beat

I don't mind you com-ing here,
I don't mind you hang-ing out

wast-ing all my
and talk-ing in your

time.
sleep.

'Cause when you're stand-ing oh, so___ near,
It does-n't mat-ter where you've___ been

Just What I Needed - 3 - 1

© 1978 LIDO MUSIC, INC.
All Rights Reserved

LAYLA

Words and Music by
ERIC CLAPTON and JIM GORDON

© 1970 (Renewed) ERIC PATRICK CLAPTON and THROAT MUSIC LTD.
All Rights Administered by WB MUSIC CORP.
All Rights Reserved

Chorus:

la,_____ you got me on___ my knees.___ Lay -

la,_____ I beg you, dar - ling, please.___ Lay -

la,_____ dar - lin', won't you ease my wor-ried

mind?_____

Repeat as desired for solos

rit. e dim.

mp

LOLA

Words and Music by
RAY DAVIES

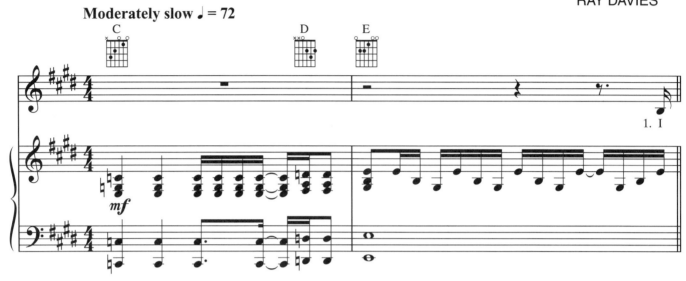

Verses 1 & 2:

met her in a club down in old So - - ho_____ where you
(2.) I'm not the world's most phys - i - cal guy,_____ but when she

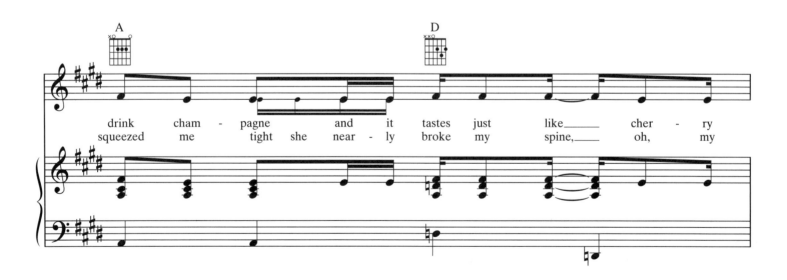

drink cham - pagne and it tastes just like_____ cher - ry
squeezed me tight she near - ly broke my spine,_____ oh, my

Lola - 6 - 1

© 1970 (Renewed) ABKCO MUSIC INC., 85 Fifth Avenue, New York, NY 10003 and DAVRAY MUSIC LTD.
All Rights for DAVRAY MUSIC LTD. Administered by UNICHAPPELL MUSIC INC.
All Rights Reserved

Bridge 2:

Lo - la.   Girls will be boys,__ and boys__ will be girls; it's a

mixed-up, mud-dled-up, shook-up world__ ex-cept for Lo - la,   Lo-lo - lo - lo

D.S. % al Coda   Coda

Lo - la.   Well,   Lo - la.__

Repeat ad lib. and fade

Lo - la,   Lo-lo - lo-lo Lo - la,   Lo-lo - lo-lo Lo - la.__

Lola - 6 - 6

MARGARITAVILLE

Words and Music by
JIMMY BUFFETT

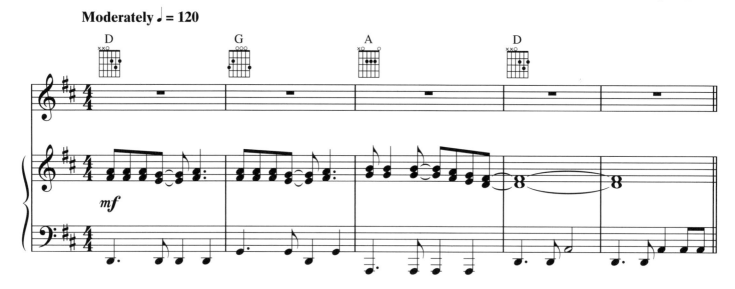

Verse:

1. Nib - blin' on sponge - cake, watch - in' the sun
2. Don't know the rea - son I stayed here all sea-
3. I blew out my flip - flop, stepped on a pop-

___ bake; all of those tour - ists cov - ered with oil.___
son with noth - ing to show___ but this brand - new tat - too.___
top; cut my heel,___ had to cruise on back home.___

Margaritaville - 4 - 1

© 1977 (Renewed) CORAL REEFER MUSIC
All Rights Reserved

3.

Yes, and some__ peo - ple claim__ that there's__ a wom - an to blame,_____ and I know__ it's my own__ damn__ fault.__

NA NA HEY HEY KISS HIM GOODBYE

Words and Music by
GARY DE CARLO, DALE FRASHUER and PAUL LEKA

With a beat

1. Na na

na na   na na na   na na,   Hey hey hey,   good - bye.
na na   na na na   na na,   Hey hey hey,   good - bye.

He'll ne - ver   love   you   the   way that I   love   you,
He's ne - ver   near   you   to com - fort and   cheer   you.

'cause if   he   did   no,   no he would-n't   make   you   cry.
When   all those   sad   tears   are _____   falling baby   from your   eyes.

Na Na Hey Hey Kiss Him Goodbye - 2 - 1

© 1969 (Renewed) UNICHAPPELL MUSIC, INC.
All Rights Reserved

Na Na Hey Hey Kiss Him Goodbye - 2 - 2

RIGHT NOW

Words and Music by
SAMMY HAGAR, ALEX VAN HALEN,
MICHAEL ANTHONY and EDWARD VAN HALEN

Right Now - 8 - 1

© 1991 CABO WABO MUSIC and VAN HALEN PUBLISHING, LLC
All Rights Administered by WB MUSIC CORP.
All Rights Reserved

Verse:

1. Don't wan - na wait___ till to - mor - row.
2. *See additional lyrics*

Why put it off an - oth - er day?___

One by one, girl, prob - lems build up___

Pre-chorus:

1. One step a-head,_ one step be-hind_ it.
2. *See additional lyrics*
(3.) now. *(Inst. solo ad lib....*

Now, you got-ta run_____ to get e-ven.

Make fu-ture plans, don't live a-bout_ yes-ter-day,_ hey!

Repeat ad lib. and fade

Verse 2:
Miss a beat, you lose the rhythm,
And nothing falls into place.
Only missed by a fraction,
Sent a little off your pace.

Pre-chorus 2:
The more things you get, the more you want,
Just tradin' one for the other.
Workin' so hard to make it easy.
Got to turn, come on, turn this thing around.
(To Chorus:)

ROUNDABOUT

Words and Music by
JON ANDERSON and STEVE HOWE

*Guitar adapted for keyboard.

Roundabout - 16 - 1

© 1972 (Renewed) TOPOGRAPHIC MUSIC LIMITED
All Rights Administered by WB MUSIC CORP.
All Rights Reserved

(Tacet 1st time; play cues 2nd and 3rd times only)

N.C.

Play 3 times

A - long the drift - ing cloud,_ the ea - gle search - ing down_ on the land.
Catch-ing the swirl-ing wind,_ the sail-or sees the rim_ of the land.
The ea-gle's danc-ing wings_ cre-ate as weath - er spins_ out of hand.

Play 3 times

Go clos-er hold the land,_ feel part - ly no more than_grains of sand.
We stand to lose all time,_ a thou-sand an-swers by_ in our hand.
Next to your deep - er fears,_ we stand sur-round-ed by a mil - lion years.

I'll be the round - a - bout; the words will make

you out and out. you out and out.

Freely, slowly

Em

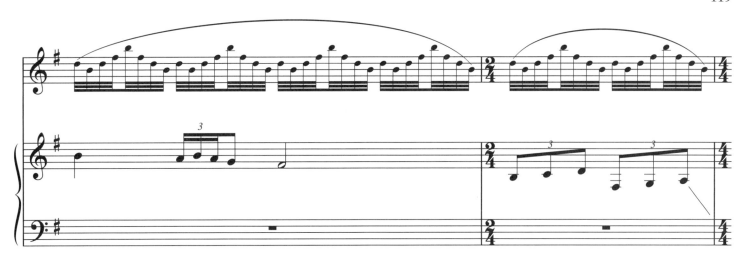

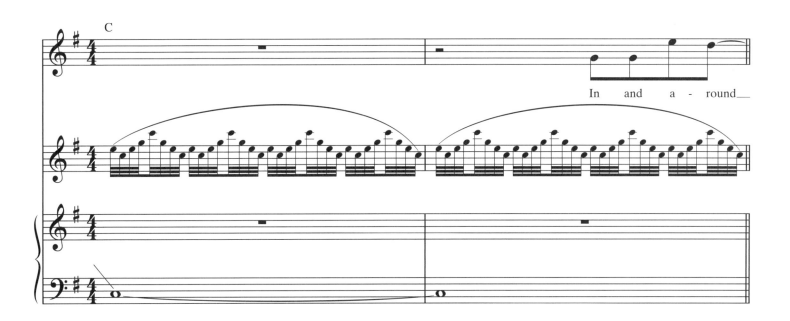

In and a - round___

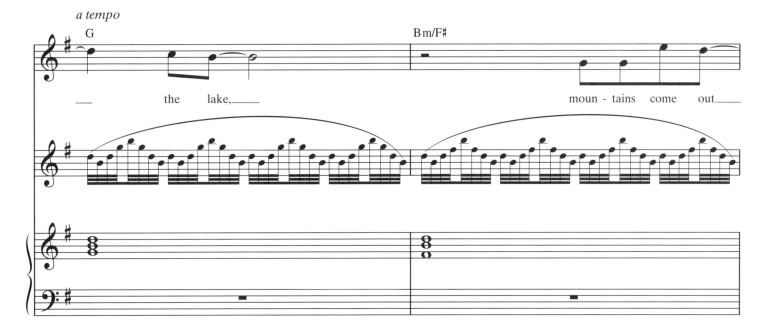

___ the lake,___

moun - tains come out___

of the sky, they stand there.

Twen-ty-four be-fore my love and I'll be there.

Organ solo:

122

RUNNING ON EMPTY

Words and Music by
JACKSON BROWNE

Running on Empty - 8 - 1

© 1977 (Renewed), 1978 SWALLOW TURN MUSIC
All Rights Reserved

Ev-'ry-one I know,___ ev-'ry-where I go,___

SHOWER THE PEOPLE

Words and Music by
JAMES TAYLOR

© 1975 (Renewed) COUNTRY ROAD MUSIC, INC.
All Rights Reserved

Vocal Ad Lib

They say in every life,
They say the rain must fall.
Just like a pouring rain,
Make it rain.
Love is sunshine.

STAIRWAY TO HEAVEN

Words and Music by
JIMMY PAGE and ROBERT PLANT

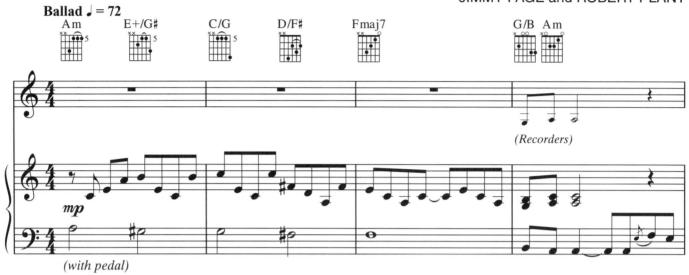

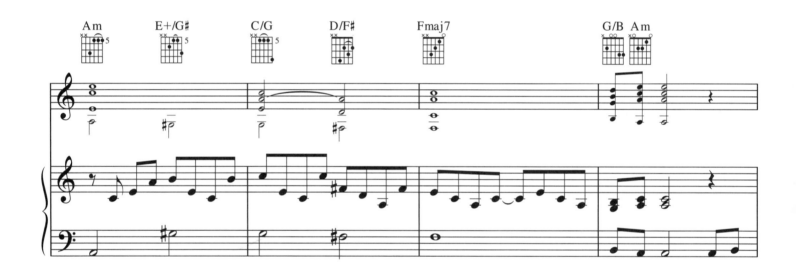

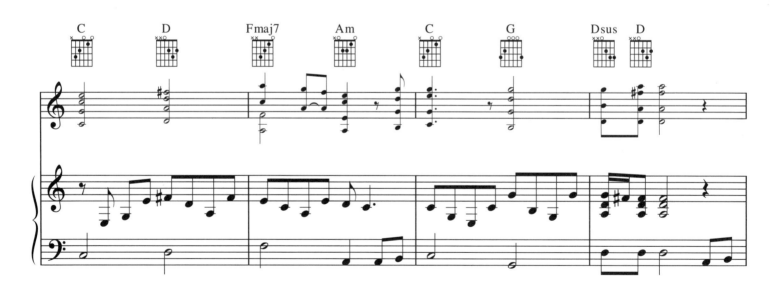

Stairway to Heaven - 12 - 1

© 1972 (Renewed) FLAMES OF ALBION MUSIC, INC.
All Rights Administered by WB MUSIC CORP.
Exclusive Print Rights for the World Excluding Europe Administered by ALFRED PUBLISHING CO., INC.
All Rights Reserved

Verses 2 & 3:

there's still time to change the road you're on.
your stair - way lies on the whis - p'rin' wind.

And it makes me won - der,

ahh.

146

SUNSHINE OF YOUR LOVE

Words and Music by
JACK BRUCE, PETE BROWN
and ERIC CLAPTON

Moderately ♩ = 102

1. It's get-ting near dawn,
(2. 4.) with you, my love,
3. (Inst. solo ad lib....

when lights close their tir-ed eyes.____ I'll
the light's shin-ing through__ on you.____ Yes, I'm

Sunshine of Your Love - 4 - 1

© 1967 (Renewed) DRATLEAF MUSIC, LTD. and E. C. MUSIC, LTD.
All Rights Administered by UNICHAPPELL MUSIC, INC.
All Rights Reserved

Repeat and fade

TAXI

Words and Music by
HARRY CHAPIN

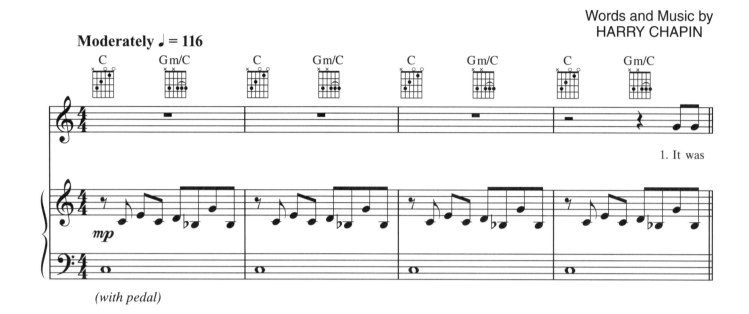

1. It was

Verse 1:

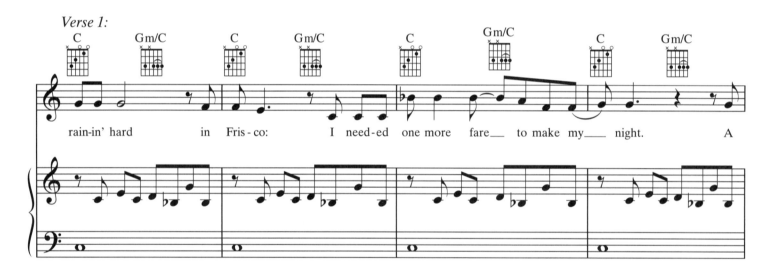

rain-in' hard in Fris-co: I need-ed one more fare___ to make my___ night. A

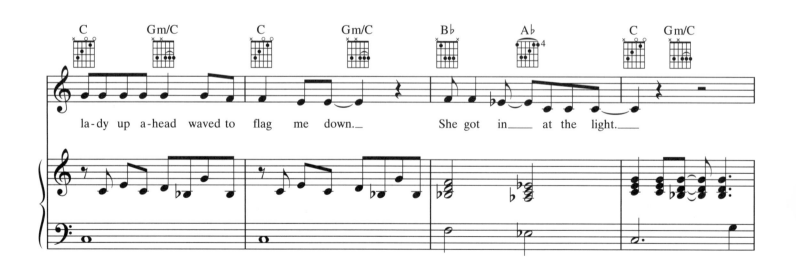

la-dy up a-head waved to flag me down.___ She got in___ at the light.___

Taxi - 12 - 1

© 1972 (Renewed) STORY SONGS, LTD.
All Rights Administered by WB MUSIC CORP.
All Rights Reserved

Verse 2:

2. "Oh, where___ you go-ing to, my La-dy Blue? It's a shame you___ ruined your___ ___ gown___ in the rain." She just looked_ out the win-dow, she said, "Six-teen Park - side Lane."

mf

% *Verses 3 & 6:*

3. Some-thing a - bout___ her was fa -
6. *See additional lyrics*

Chorus:

And she said, "How_ are you, Har-ry?" I_____ said, "How are you, Sue?_

__ Through the too man-y miles_ and the too lit-tle smiles,_ I still_____

__ re-mem-ber you."

Verse 5:

5. It was some-where in a fair-y-tale; I used to take her home in my car. We learned a-bout love in the back of a Dodge; the les-son had-n't gone too far.____

Chorus:

You see, she was gon-na be an ac - tress, and I was gon-na learn to fly.____ She took off____ to find the

Outro:

fly - ing so___ high___ when I'm___

stoned.___

Repeat ad lib. and fade

Verse 6:
There was not much more for us to talk about;
Whatever we had once was gone.
So I turned my cab into the driveway,
Past the gate and the fine-trimmed lawns.

Verse 7:
And she said, "We must get together,"
But I knew it'd never be arranged.
Then she handed me twenty dollars for a two-fifty fare;
She said, *(spoken)* "Harry, keep the change."
(To Verse 8:)

TIME OF THE SEASON

Words and Music by
ROD ARGENT

Moderately ♩ = 116

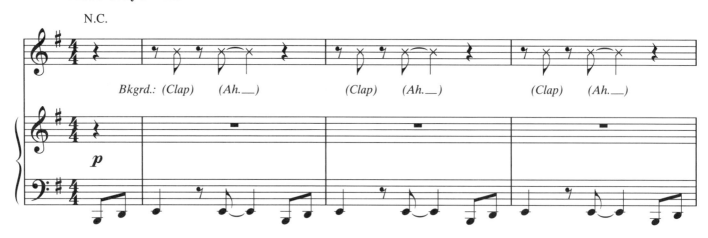

Verse 1:

Time of the Season - 4 - 1

© 1967 (Renewed) VERULAM MUSIC CO., LTD.
All Rights for the U.S. and Canada Controlled by MAINSTAY MUSIC, INC.
All Rights Reserved

and let me try___ with pleas-ured hands___ to take you in the

...end Bkgrd.)

cresc. **mf**

sun to prom-ised lands,___ to show you ev-'ry one.___ It's the time___

f

N.C.

Am7   E/B

N.C.

___ of the sea - son for lov - ing.

Bkgrd.: (Clap) (Ah.__) (Clap) (Ah.__) (Clap) (Ah.__) (Clap) (Ah.__)

2. What's your name?__

Verses 2, 3, & 4:

LIKE A ROLLING STONE

Words and Music by
BOB DYLAN

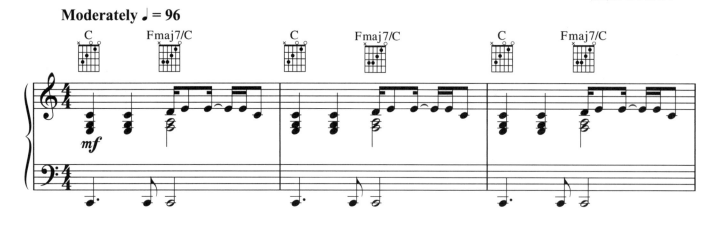

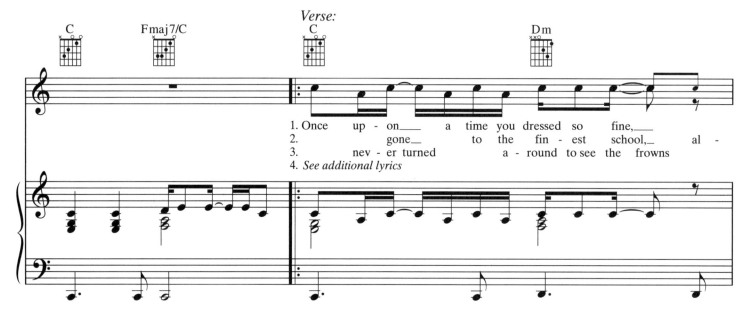

Verse:

1. Once up-on___ a time you dressed so fine,___
2. ___ gone___ to the fin-est school,___ al -
3. ___ nev-er turned a-round to see the frowns
4. *See additional lyrics*

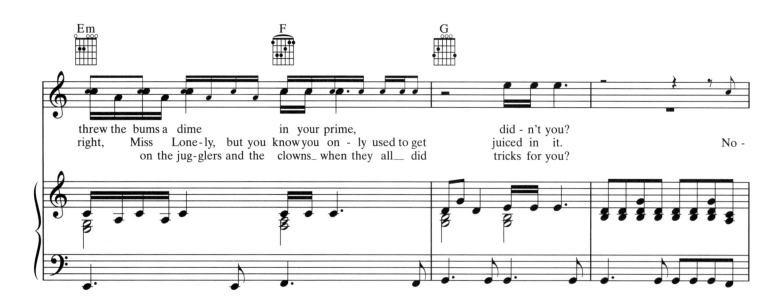

threw the bums a dime ___ in your prime, ___ did-n't you?
right, Miss Lone-ly, but you know you on-ly used to get juiced in it.
on the jug-glers and the clowns___ when they all___ did tricks for you? No-

Like a Rolling Stone - 5 - 1

© 1965 (Renewed) SPECIAL RIDER MUSIC
Used by Permission of MUSIC SALES CORPORATION (ASCAP)
All Rights Reserved

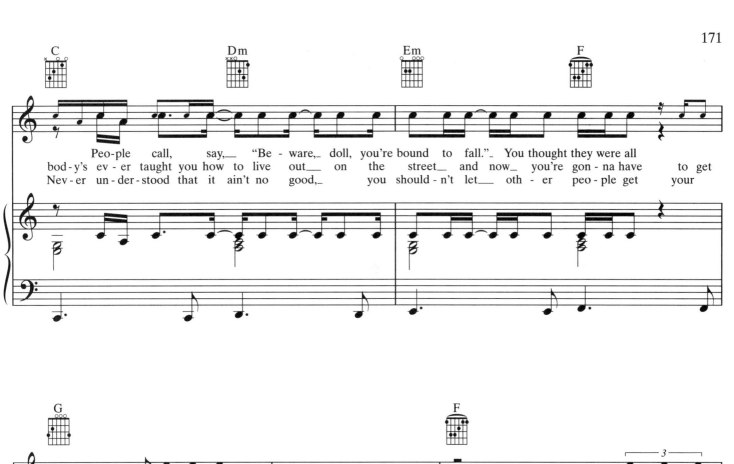

C   Dm   Em   F

Peo-ple call, say,__ "Be-ware,_ doll, you're bound to fall."_ You thought they were all
bod-y's ev-er taught you how to live out__ on the street__ and now__ you're gon-na have to get
Nev-er un-der-stood that it ain't no good,__ you should-n't let__ oth-er peo-ple get your

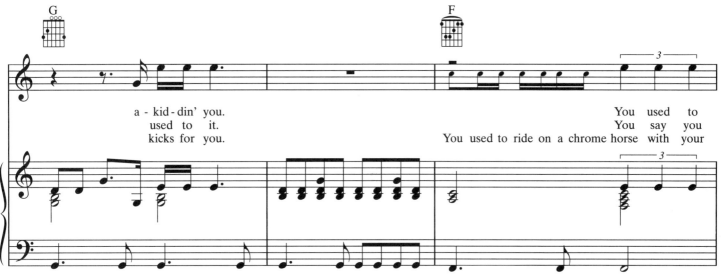

G   F

a - kid-din' you.
used to it.
kicks for you.
            You used to
            You say you
            You used to ride on a chrome horse with your

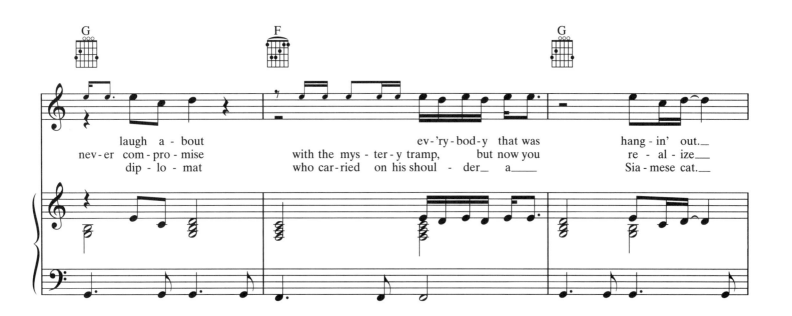

G   F   G

laugh a - bout
nev-er com-pro-mise
dip - lo - mat
      ev-'ry-bod-y that was
      with the mys - ter-y tramp,
      who car-ried on his shoul - der__ a____
      hang-in' out.__
      but now you re - al - ize__
      Sia-mese cat.__

4.

like__ a com-plete un - known,__ like a roll - ing stone?__

1.2.3. etc.   *Repeat and fade* | Optional ending

Verse 4:
Princess on the steeple and all the pretty people,
They're all drinkin', thinkin' that they got it made.
Exchanging all precious gifts,
But you better take your diamond ring,
You'd better pawn it, babe.
You used to be so amused
At Napolean in rags and the language that he used.
Go to him now, he calls you, you can't refuse.
When you got nothin', you got nothin' to lose.
You're invisible now, you got no secrets to conceal.
(*To Chorus:*)

TOM SAWYER

Words by
PYE DUBOIS and NEIL PEART

Music by
GEDDY LEE and ALEX LIFESON

Tom Sawyer - 7 - 1

© 1981 CORE MUSIC PUBLISHING
All Rights Reserved

N.C.

What you say___ a-bout his com-pa-ny___ is
And what you say___ a-bout his com-pa-ny___ is

what you say___ a-bout so-ci-e-ty.___ Catch the mist,___
what you say___ a-bout so-ci-e-ty.___ Catch the wit-ness,

catch the myth,___ catch the mys-t'ry, catch the drift.___
catch the wit,___ catch the spir-it, catch the spit.___

day's Tom Saw-yer, he gets high on you,__ and the space he in - vades,__ he gets by___ on you.

Guitar solo ad lib.

D.S. ℅ al Coda

THE TREES

Words by
NEIL PEART

Music by
GEDDY LEE and ALEX LIFESON

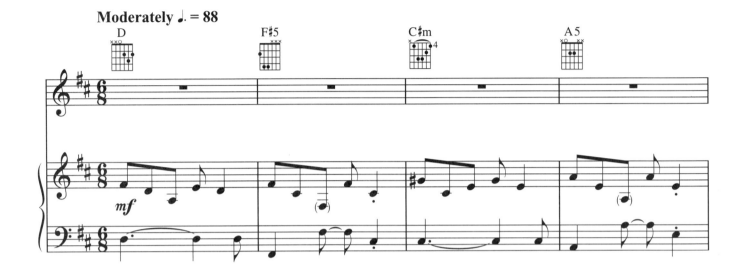

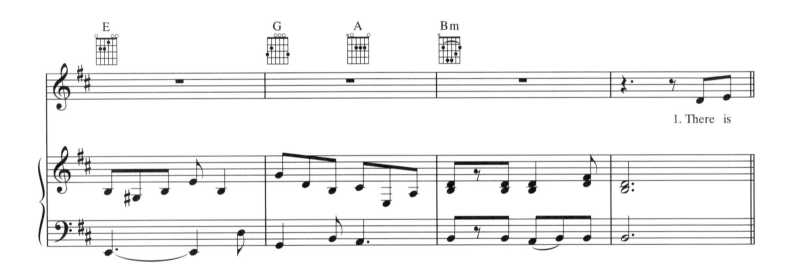

Verse 1:

The Trees - 10 - 1

© 1978 CORE MUSIC PUBLISHING
All Rights Reserved

Ma - ples want more sun - light and the Oaks ig - nore their pleas.

Moderately fast rock ♩ = 138

(♪=♪)

The

Guitar solo ad lib.

(end ad lib. solo)

UNCLE JOHN'S BAND

Words by
ROBERT HUNTER

Music by
JERRY GARCIA

Well, the first days— are— the hard-est days;— don't you
buck danc-er's— choice— my friend;— bet-ter

wor-ry an-y-more. 'Cause— when life— looks like Eas-y Street,there is
take— my— ad-vice. You know— all the rules by now— and the

Uncle John's Band - 7 - 1

© 1970 (Renewed) ICE NINE PUBLISHING CO., INC.
All Rights Reserved

dan - ger at __ your door.
fire __ from __ the ice.
Think this through with me; __
Will you come __ with me? __

Let me know __ your mind. __
Won't you come __ with me? __
Wo, oh, __ what I want __ to know _____
Wo, oh, __ what I want __ to know: _____

__ is, __ are __ you kind?
__ will __ you __ come with me?
It's a

God damn, well I __ de - clare, __ have you seen the like? __

the same sto - ry the crow told me, — it's the on - ly one — he knows.
I live in a sil - ver mine — and I call it Beg - gar's Tomb.

Like the morn - ing — sun you come — and —
I got — me a vi - o - lin — and I

like the wind — you go.
beg you call — the tune.

Ain't no time — to hate, —
An - y - bod - y's choice, —

bare - ly time — to wait. —
I can hear — your voice. —

Uncle John's Band - 7 - 4

196

here be-side the ris - ing tide._ Come hear Un-

cle John's Band _ play-ing to the tide._ Come on a-long or go_

_ a - lone,_ he's come to take his chil - dren home._

Da da da da — da da, da da da da _ da da.

THE WEIGHT

Words and Music by
ROBBIE ROBERTSON

Moderately slow ♩ = 72

N.C.

Verse:

A   A   C♯m

1. I pulled in - to Naz - a - reth,   was
2.–5. *See additional lyrics*

D   A   C♯m

feel - in' 'bout half past dead.   I just need some-place___ where

D   A   C♯m

I___ can lay___ my head.___   "Hey, mis-ter, can you tell me where a

© 1968, 1974 (Copyrights Renewed) DWARF MUSIC
Used by Permission of MUSIC SALES CORPORATION (ASCAP)
All Rights Reserved

Verse 2:
I picked up my bag, I went lookin' for a place to hide,
When I saw Carmen and the devil walkin' side by side.
I said, "Hey, Carmen, come on, let's go downtown."
He said, "I gotta go, but my friend can stick around."
(To Chorus:)

Verse 3:
Go down, Miss Moses, there's nothing that you can say.
It's just old Luke and Luke's waitin' on the Judgment Day.
I said, "Luke, my friend, what about young Anna Lee?"
He said, "Do me a favor, son, won't you stay and keep Anna Lee company."
(To Chorus:)

Verse 4:
Crazy Chester followed me and he caught me in the fog.
He said, "I'll fix your rack if you'll take Jack, my dog."
I said, "Wait a minute, Chester, you know I'm a peaceful man."
He said, "That's okay, boy, won't you feed him when you can."
(To Chorus:)

Verse 5:
Catch a cannonball, now, take me down the line.
My bag is sinkin' low and I do believe it's time
To get back to Miss Fanny, you know she's the only one
Who sent me here with her regards for everyone.
(To Chorus:)

WHIPPING POST

Words and Music by
GREGG ALLMAN

Moderately fast ♪ = 212

N.C.

1. I been

Whipping Post - 6 - 1

© 1970 (Renewed) UNICHAPPELL MUSIC, INC. and ELIJAH BLUE MUSIC
All Rights Reserved

Chorus:

Verse 2:
My friends tell me that I've been such a fool,
And I had to stand by and take it, baby, all for lovin' you.
I drown myself in sorrow, as I look at what you've done,
But nothin' seems to change, the bad times stay the same, and I cannot run.
(To Chorus:)

WEREWOLVES OF LONDON

Words and Music by
WARREN ZEVON, WADDY WACHTEL
and LEROY MARINELL

© 1975 (Renewed) ZEVON MUSIC, LEADSHEET LAND MUSIC and TINY TUNES
All Rights Reserved

Werewolves of London - 7 - 2

Verse 3:

hair - y - head - ed gent who ran a - muck in Kent._

Late - ly he's been o - ver-heard in May - fair.

You bet - ter stay a - way from him. *He'll rip your lungs out, Jim.*

D.S. %al Coda

Huh! I'd like to meet his tai - lor.

A WHITER SHADE OF PALE

Words and Music by
KEITH REID and GARY BROOKER

Moderately slow ♩ = 76

Verse:

1. We skipped the light fan - dan - go,___
2. She said, "There is no rea - son,___

A Whiter Shade of Pale - 5 - 1

TRO - © 1967 (Renewed) WESTMINSTER MUSIC LTD., London, England
TRO-ESSEX MUSIC, INC., New York, Controls all Publication Rights for the U.S. and Canada
All Rights Reserved   Used by Permission

216

A Whiter Shade of Pale - 5 - 3

And so it

YOU CAN LEAVE YOUR HAT ON

Words and Music by
RANDY NEWMAN

Moderate rock ♩ = 92

You Can Leave Your Hat On - 6 - 1

© 1972, 1976 (Copyrights Renewed) WB MUSIC CORP. and RANDY NEWMAN MUSIC
All Rights Administered by WB MUSIC CORP.
All Rights Reserved

222

YOU CAN'T ALWAYS GET WHAT YOU WANT

Guitar in Open E tuning *(optional w/ Capo at 8th fret):*

⑥ = E ③ = G#
⑤ = B ② = B
④ = E ① = E

Words and Music by
MICK JAGGER and
KEITH RICHARDS

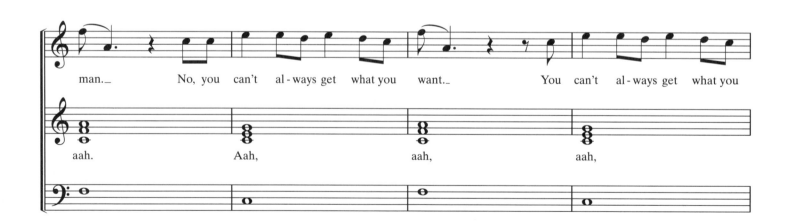

You Can't Always Get What You Want - 10 - 1

© 1969 (Renewed) ABKCO MUSIC, INC., 85 Fifth Avenue, New York, NY 10003
All Rights Reserved

228

(Lead Vocal) 1. I

%§ Verses 1 & 5:

saw her to-day___ at the re-cep - tion,
5. See additional lyrics

a glass of wine_____ in her hand._____ I knew_

___ she was gon - na meet her con-nec - tion._____ At her

Chorus:

230

You Can't Always Get What You Want - 10 - 8

Repeat ad lib. and fade

Verse 3:
I went down to the Chelsea drugstore
To get your prescription filled.
I was standin' in line with Mr. Jimmy.
A-man, did he look pretty ill.

Verse 4:
We decided that we would have a soda;
My favorite flavor, cherry red,
I sung my song to Mr. Jimmy.
Yeah, and he said one word to me, and that was "dead."
I said to him…
(To Chorus:)

Verse 5:
I saw her today at the reception.
In her glass was a bleeding man.
She was practiced at the art of deception.
Well, I could tell by her blood-stained hands.
Say it!
(To Chorus:)

WISH YOU WERE HERE

Words and Music by
ROGER WATERS and DAVID GILMOUR

Slow rock feel (= 63)

(2nd time - Acoustic Guitar solo ad lib.)

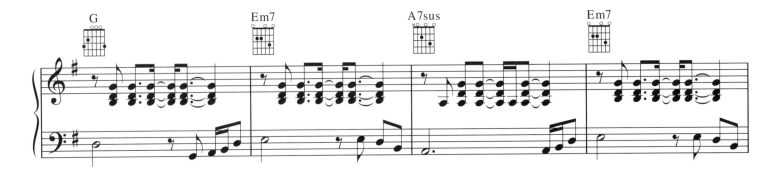

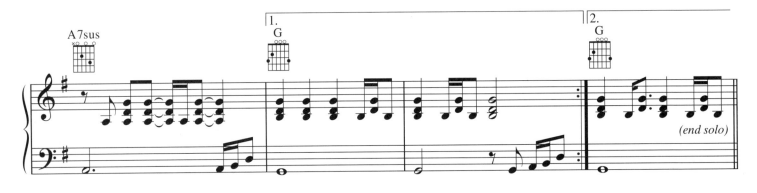

(end solo)

Verse 1:

So,_____ so you think you can tell_____ heav-en from hell,__

© 1975 (Renewed) ROGER WATERS OVERSEAS LTD. and PINK FLOYD MUSIC PUBLISHERS, INC.
All Rights for ROGER WATERS OVERSEAS LTD. in the U.S and Canada Administered by WARNER-TAMERLANE PUBLISHING CORP.
All Rights Reserved

240